A NOTE TO PARENTS

When your children are ready to "step into reading," giving them the right books—and lots of them—is as crucial as giving them the right food to eat. **Step into Reading Books** present exciting stories and information reinforced with lively, colorful illustrations that make learning to read fun, satisfying, and worthwhile. They are priced so that acquiring an entire library of them is affordable. And they are beginning readers with an important difference—they're written on four levels.

Step 1 Books, with their very large type and extremely simple vocabulary, have been created for the very youngest readers. **Step 2 Books** are both longer and slightly more difficult. **Step 3 Books,** written to mid-second-grade reading levels, are for the child who has acquired even greater reading skills. **Step 4 Books** offer exciting nonfiction for the increasingly proficient reader.

Children develop at different ages. **Step into Reading Books,** with their four levels of reading, are designed to help children become good—and interested—readers *faster*. The grade levels assigned to the four steps—preschool through grade 1 for Step 1, grades 1 through 3 for Step 2, grades 2 and 3 for Step 3, and grades 2 through 4 for Step 4—are intended only as guides. Some children move through all four steps very rapidly; others climb the steps over a period of several years. These books will help your child "step into reading" in style!

To Justin, Jennifer, Sunny,
and Bob's pool

—J. M.

To Bill and Carol—
Thanks. Love, Mom

—B. S.

Library of Congress Cataloging-in-Publication Data: Marzollo, Jean. Cannonball Chris.
(Step into reading. A step 3 book) SUMMARY: Chris tries to overcome his fear of jumping
into deep water in time for the second-grade swimming party. [1. Fear–Fiction. 2.
Swimming–Fiction] I. Sims, Blanche, ill. II. Title. III. Series: Step into reading. Step
3 book. PZ7.M3688Can 1987 [E] 86-31512 ISBN: 0-394-88512-0 (pbk.); 0-394-98512-5
(lib. bdg.)

Manufactured in the United States of America   12   13   14   15   16   17   18   19   20

STEP INTO READING is a trademark of Random House, Inc.

Step into Reading

CANNONBALL CHRIS

by Jean Marzollo
illustrated by Blanche Sims

A Step 3 Book

Random House New York

Chapter 1

It was a hot summer day. Chris was
at the town pool with all his friends.
He was fooling around and making them
laugh.

"Guess what I am?" he shouted. Then
he floated on his back and spouted water.

"A whale!" cried Tommy. He copied
Chris. So did the other kids. Chris was
the biggest—and silliest—of all the
second graders.

Chris was so big and so silly that he seemed to have no fear. But he <u>was</u> afraid of something. And it was a secret.

Chris was afraid of the deep end of the town pool. He could swim in deep water. That was no problem. But he could not jump into it. He was afraid that if he did, he would not come up again.

Chris went swimming all summer long. But he never told anyone his secret.

One day he was at the pool with his friends. They were doing cannonballs off the diving board.

"Come on, Chris," said Billy. "You're so big, you'll make the biggest splash of all."

Chris swam quickly to the shallow end
and got out. "Watch!" he cried. "This is
even better! A twirl bomb!"

Chris twirled and did a cannonball into the shallow end of the pool. He made a big splash and jumped up. The other kids laughed. They came down to the shallow end and copied Chris's twirl bomb.

Chris wanted to keep everyone at the shallow end. So he invented another cannonball: the buzz bomb. He buzzed like a dive bomber and jumped into the pool.

He invented the bear bomb, too. He roared like a bear as he jumped.

Then he invented the popcorn
cannonball. He hopped up and down at the
edge of the pool like popcorn popping in
a hot pan. "Pop! Pop! Pop!" he cried as
he jumped into the pool.

All the kids laughed. And they all
copied Chris's funny cannonballs. They
never knew that Chris was staying at the
shallow end on purpose.

Chapter 2

A few days later Chris got a letter in the mail. It was an invitation to Tommy's birthday party. It said, "Swim party! Bring your bathing suit."

Chris called Tommy on the phone to say he could come.

"Great," said Tommy. "There's going to be a cannonball contest off the diving board. You'll probably win."

That night Chris had a nightmare. He dreamed that he was at Tommy's party. He was standing on the diving board. Everyone was waiting for him to jump.

"Jump! Jump!" they yelled.

Chris didn't want to do it, but he had to. Down he went. His feet never touched bottom. He was falling into a dark, endless pit. "Help!" he cried.

Chris woke up in a sweat.

His father came into his room and sat down on Chris's bed. "What's the matter?" he asked.

"I had a terrible dream," said Chris. He told his father about it.

"Everyone's afraid of something," said his father. "You're afraid of deep water. How do you think you can solve this problem?"

Chris shivered. "By not going to Tommy's party," he said.

His dad smiled. He said, "I have a better idea. Tomorrow I'll tell you about the Dirt Road Bear."

"What's that?" asked Chris.

"That's what I was afraid of once," said his dad.

Chapter 3

The next day Chris and his dad drove
to the state park. They rented a canoe
and paddled around the lake.

"When I was little," said Chris's dad,
"I was afraid of dirt roads. I thought
bears lived on them. So my dad took me
out into the country. He had me sit on
a rock at the beginning of a dirt road.

"'When I am out of sight,' he said, 'count to a hundred. Then follow me.' Then he walked down the road until I couldn't see him anymore.

"Well, I counted to a hundred. I was really scared. I hated to walk down that road alone. I was sure bears were waiting to jump out at me.

"But somehow I did it. And at the end
of the road I saw my dad. I ran up
and hugged him.

"'I am very proud of you,' he said.
I felt so brave! And I was never afraid
of dirt roads again."

"Did you see a bear?" asked Chris.

"Not a one," said his father. "My dad
said there weren't any. He was right."

Chapter 4

Chris thought about his dad's story. After a while he and his dad returned the canoe. Then they walked past the state park swimming pool.

"Part of the trick is to name your fear. I named mine the Dirt Road Bear," said Chris's dad. "What do you call yours?"

"The Underwater Pit," said Chris. "I'm afraid that if I jump into it, I'll never come out."

He and his dad were quiet. Then his dad said, "If you want to try now, I'll catch you. I'll be in the water, waiting."

Chris was nervous. But he said okay. A few minutes later he stood at the end of the diving board. He felt sick.

"Count to three and jump," said his dad.

"One...two...three," said Chris. He jumped off the board. He felt dark fear and water all around him. He was going straight down into the pit! Then he felt his father's strong arms.

"Now try it again," said his father. "This time jump in with your arms up. When you are in the water, pull your arms down. You'll pop up like a cork."

Chris stood on the diving board again. "I don't think I'll pop up like a cork," he said. "I think I'll go down into the pit like a rock."

"If you do, I'll pull you up," said his dad. "Trust me."

Chris put up his arms and jumped. His body dropped through the water. He pulled his arms down to his sides. SPLASH! Up he popped!

"You did it!" said his dad.

Chris had never felt happier.

"I'm going to do that again!" he said.
Chris jumped off the diving board ten more
times.

"Now I'm going to sit on the edge of
the pool," said his dad. "You don't need
me anymore."

For a moment Chris was scared.
Then he had an idea. "I'm going to do
a cannonball," he said.

Chris stood at the back of the diving
board. His dad sat on the edge of the
pool. Chris ran and jumped in. In the
air he pulled his feet up and held them
with his arms. He made a splash so big,
his dad got all wet.

"There is no Underwater Pit," Chris said on the way home.

"I know," said his dad. "I'm proud of you."

Chris was proud of himself too. But somewhere inside him was a little worry. What about Tommy's pool? His dad wouldn't be with him at the party.

"I wish you could come to Tommy's party with me," said Chris.

His father smiled. "You'll be okay," he said. "You'll see."

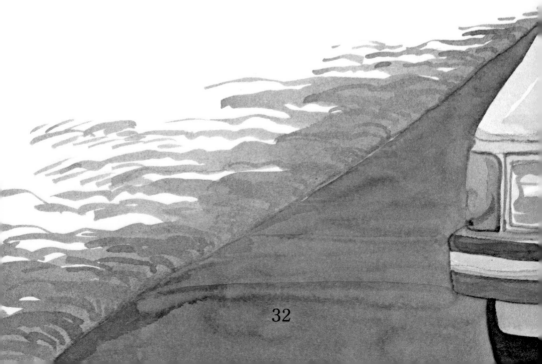

Chapter 5

The day of the party came. All the kids
were swimming in Tommy's pool. They were
having a great time. Except for Chris.
His old fear was back. He kept on
thinking, "Maybe there's an Underwater Pit
in Tommy's pool." And he knew the
cannonball contest would be starting soon.

Then Tommy's mother held up a huge squirt gun. "Whoever does the best cannonball off the diving board wins this," she said.

"Me first!" called everyone except Chris.

"Tommy is first," said his mother. "He's the birthday boy. The rest of you line up behind him."

Chris was last in line.

Tommy gave a big jump. He was small. His cannonball was small too.

Freddy did a flip cannonball. He landed on his side.

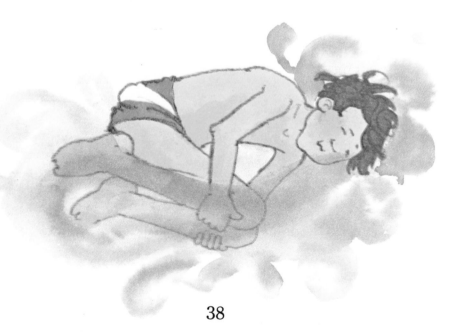

Billy ran and jumped so fast that he did a belly flop.

Rosie did a twirl cannonball. It was only so-so.

"Watch me!" said Sally. She ran and jumped way out into the pool. She went farther than anyone.

"That was pretty good," said Billy.

"Watch Chris," said Tommy. "He'll do one of his funny dives."

Chris stood at the back of the board. He kept telling himself what his father had said: People always pop up like corks. Tommy, Billy, Freddy, Rosie, and Sally had all popped up. Right? Right.

"This is a special combination buzz-bear bomb," said Chris.

He ran down the board, buzzing like a dive bomber. He jumped into the air and grabbed his legs. "Grrr!" he roared. Then he hit the water with a giant splash.

Down he went. Quickly he pulled his
arms to his sides. His body shot up. His
head popped out of the water.

"You win!" everyone shouted.
Chris climbed out of the pool.

Tommy's mother gave him the prize squirt gun. It was already filled with water. Chris squirted everyone—except Tommy's mother. Then he squirted the diving board. "Take that!" he said. "I'm the cannonball king!"